Octopus or Squid?

A Compare and Contrast Book

by AnnMarie Lisi

Octopuses and squids don't have backbones like we do. They are invertebrates.

They live in saltwater and are found from coastal reefs to deep water habitats in tropical and temperate waters.

Octopuses have eight arms
covered in suction cups.

Squids have eight arms and
two long tentacles covered in
suction cups and hooks.

Octopuses have small bodies, called mantles, and huge heads.

Squids have long mantles with fins and small triangle-shaped heads.

Octopuses' strong arms let them "walk" on the ocean floor. They can use their arms to hold onto and move objects.

Both have mouths in the middle of their arms. The mouths have a beak-like structure to crush and tear their food.

All octopuses and some squids use venom to kill their prey. The venom of the small blue ring octopus is harmful to humans.

Both squid and octopuses can swim by sucking water into their mantles and pushing it out a siphon.

They have large, complex eyes. Scientists think they "see" color in ways that no other animal can. That helps them to be masters of camouflage.

Octopuses have rectangle-shaped pupils. Squid have round-shaped pupils.

Octopuses and squids have special skin cells that change the color and texture of their skin to look like objects in their habitat.

That's a great way to hide from predators and to sneak up on prey!

The mimic octopus has even been seen changing its color and texture to look like, or mimic, other animals.

Octopuses are usually solitary animals
that live on or near the ocean floor,
hiding in caves and crevices.

Squid live alone or in groups.
They swim in open waters.

A female octopus lays eggs in a strand-like pattern in her den. She protects them until they hatch.

Female squids attach eggs
to things and swim away.

When scared, octopuses and squids both shoot ink out through their siphons into the water to protect themselves. The cloud of inky water confuses their predators and gives them time to escape.

There are around 300 species of octopuses.

The largest is the giant pacific octopus. It can average 16 feet (more than 4 meters) in length and weigh about 100 pounds (45 kilograms).

How tall are you and how much do you weight?

There are also around 300 species of squid ranging in size from 1 inch (2 ½ centimeters) to over 43 feet (13 meters) long.

For Creative Minds

Cephalopods

Animals like fish, birds, reptiles, amphibians, and mammals all have backbones and are called vertebrates. Animals that do not have backbones are invertebrates. Insects and mollusks are invertebrates. There are almost 100,000 different kinds of mollusks, including snails and slugs. Some marine mollusks you might recognize are clams, oysters, and scallops.

Octopuses and squids belong to a group of marine mollusks called cephalopods which means "head-foot." Their arms attach straight to their heads! Other cephalopods include cuttlefish and nautiluses.

Octopuses have eight arms. Squids and cuttlefishes have a combination of ten arms and tentacles. Nautiluses have up to 90 arms that don't have suckers but do have sticky grooves to grab prey.

octopus

squid

cuttlefish

nautilus

Fun Facts

Both octopuses and squids eat meat (carnivores). They grab prey with their arms (or tentacles). They use their suction cups to see if the animal tastes like something they should eat or not. If so, they carry the prey towards their mouth and use their strong beaks to tear meat into small pieces to eat.

Octopuses prey on crabs, lobsters, snails, and other shellfish.

Squids prey on fish and shrimp.

Squid beaks are so strong, they are sometimes found undigested inside the stomachs of their predators.

Octopuses and squids have 3 hearts and blue blood. They breathe oxygen from the water through gills.

Octopuses and squids can regrow an arm (but not a tentacle) if they lose one.

Some types of squids can swim as fast as 25 miles (40 km) per hour in short bursts.

Compared to its body size, a squid's eye is very large. A giant squid's eyes are about the size of a soccer ball!

Octopuses are extremely smart. They have been known to "break out" of their exhibits at zoos or aquariums and wander around.

Because they don't have any bones, they can squeeze through small holes and can use their suction cups to climb up or down.

Some zoos or aquariums put carpeting or AstroTurf around octopus exhibits because the suction cups can't hold onto that material to get out!

Who Am I?

Using information learned in the book, see if you can identify which animal is which.

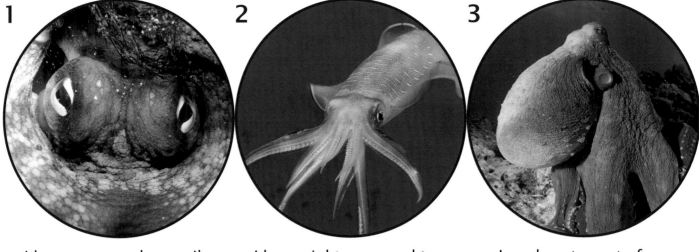

1 I have rectangular pupils.

2 I have eight arms and two tentacles.

3 I push water out of my siphon to help me swim.

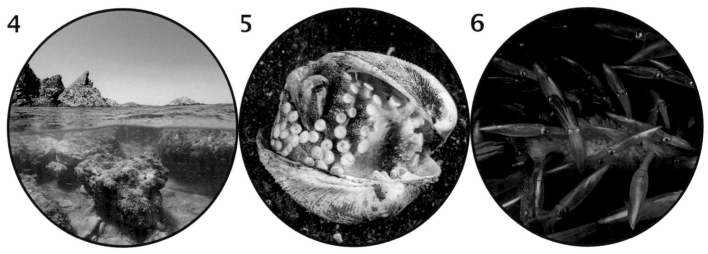

4 I live in saltwater in warm or temperate climates.

5 I sometimes walk on my arms. I can also hold onto and move things with my arms. I can even move shells and rocks around to make a den.

6 I may live in large groups.

Octopus: 1-rectangular pupils, 5-arms
Squid: 2-8 arms & 2 tentacles, 6-large groups
Both: 3-siphon, 4-saltwater habitat

Match the Adaptations

Match the photograph to its description.

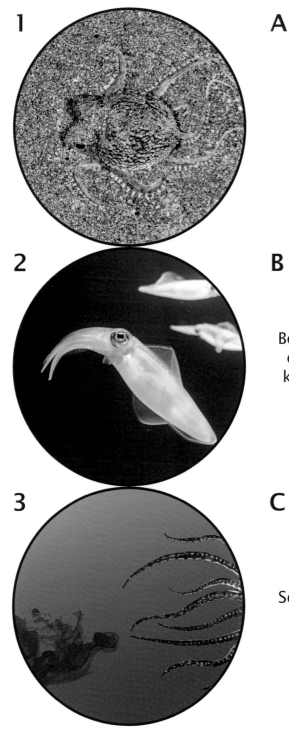

1

A

Both octopuses and squids release dark ink clouds to confuse would-be predators. The ink prevents the predators from seeing them swim away.

2

B

Both octopuses and squids change the color and texture of their skins to camouflage themselves. This helps to keep them safe from predators. It also helps them hide from the prey they want to catch to eat.

3

C

Squids have long mantles with fins that help move them through the water.

1-B; 2-C, 3-A

I would like to dedicate this book to my two daughters, Madelyn and Ella. May you always be curious, appreciate nature, and make the environment a better place for all—AML

Thanks to Sarena Randall Gill, PhD, environmental educator and member of the board of the National Association for Interpretation for verifying the information in this book.

Thanks to the South Carolina Aquarium for the use of the photo showing the back of the octopus exhibit. All other photographs are licensed through Adobe Stock Photos or Shutterstock.

Library of Congress Cataloging-in-Publication Data

Names: Lisi, AnnMarie, 1985- author.
Title: Octopus or squid? : a compare and contrast book / by AnnMarie Lisi.
Description: Mt. Pleasant, SC : Arbordale Publishing, LLC, [2023] |
    Includes bibliographical references.
Identifiers: LCCN 2022036990 (print) | LCCN 2022036991 (ebook) | ISBN
    9781643519869 (paperback) | ISBN 9781638170051 (interactive
    dual-language, read along) | ISBN 9781638170433 (epub) | ISBN
    9781638170242 (adobe pdf)
Subjects: LCSH: Octopuses--Juvenile literature. | Squids--Juvenile
    literature.
Classification: LCC QL430.3.O2 L57 2023 (print) | LCC QL430.3.O2 (ebook)
    | DDC 594/.56--dc23/eng/20220803
LC record available at https://lccn.loc.gov/2022036990
LC ebook record available at https://lccn.loc.gov/2022036991

Translated into Spanish: *¿Pulpo o calamar? Un libro de comparaciones y contrastes*
Spanish paperback ISBN: 9781638172666
Spanish ePub ISBN: 9781638172840
Spanish PDF ebook ISBN: 9781638172840
Dual-language read-along available online at www.fathomreads.com

English Lexile® Level: 840L

Bibliography

Bradford, Alina. "Octopus Facts." Live Science, Live Science, 8 June 2017, www.livescience.com/55478-octopus-facts.html.
"Cephalopods." Smithsonian Ocean, 18 Dec. 2018, ocean.si.edu/ocean-life/invertebrates/cephalopods.
"Facts about Squids - Squid Facts and Information." Squid-World.com, 2013, www.squid-world.com/facts-about-squids/.
"The ABCs of Cephalopods with Conservation Biologist Samantha Cheng." Www.youtube.com, www.youtube.com/watch?v=EaOnTOhj-NU.
"Top 15 Facts about Squids - Vision, Shapes, Features & More." Facts.net, 8 Sept. 2017, facts.net/nature/animals/squid-facts/.
Wood, James B. "Octopus, Squid, Cuttlefish, and Nautilus - the Cephalopod Page." Thecephalopodpage.org, thecephalopodpage.org/.
Zielinski, Sarah. "Fourteen Fun Facts about Squid, Octopuses and Other Cephalopods." Smithsonian Magazine, www.smithsonianmag.com/science-nature/fourteen-fun-facts-about-squid-octopuses-and-other-cephalopods-45444510/#:~:text=Here%20are%2014%20fun%20and%20random%20facts%20I.

Arbordale Publishing, LLC
Mt. Pleasant, SC 29464
www.ArbordalePublishing.com